Daydream Dialogues

Ashley Guava

BookLeaf
Publishing

India | USA | UK

Presentation by *BookLeaf Publishing*

Web: www.bookleafpub.com

E-mail: info@bookleafpub.com

ISBN: 9789357445702

First edition 2022

This story's beginning starts in the middle.

"So how did you get here?"

"It's a little hard to say, I've
never actually had to recount this
part of the story.
Remembering is a rather peculiar sensation
at this point."

"You count remembering as a sensation?"

"Sure."

"A sensation is to be felt by the physical
senses."

"Well, then let remembering be felt
physically by the body of
my mind."

*Their eyes closed after that, as if it shut itself
in order to adhere to this 'other'
    body.*

                "Or my spirit, or whatever
                it is you believe holds the map to
                    meet remembrance."

"Where does the map lead exactly?"

                "To the crossroads of
                course. It's where we find ourselves
                    now."

*They wondered how they found themselves
in this position, unsure of
    everything they perceived. They stayed
there, like that for a few moments.
    Each staring at the other, unblinking, in the
midst of this chance encounter.*

perception

Perception, perception, perception.
Through whose eyes am I seeing
at any given time?
If I am a mosaic of all I've consumed, all I've
seen, and all those who I've come in contact
with,
Which lens is truly mine?
Or is it the combination of it all amongst the
infinite possibilities that manifested itself in me,
A lens all on its own?
Perception or reflection?

dawn

Silence.
The contentment in the early morning;
The magic of existing purely to exist;
A natural state.
When it's a little dark and the sun rises and it
becomes a little easier for me
to breathe, reflect, cleanse, direct energy
toward creating, sharing, learning, appreciating
seeing beauty with no outside demands.
Peace in the stillness of the world not quite
being fully awake.
In this moment I do not search, for I belong.
Let me be forever conscious of this state of
being.

air

Did you know that we're constantly enveloped
in air?
Presently aware that we glide through it
as if it were nothing?
The moving wind bristles over the world
saying ever eloquently that it has never left.

It whispers in between interlocked hands
    I'm here,
      We are connected in the same way.
How a small gesture can mean so much,
an expression of support, protection, affection,
connection.

One step forward,
One step back.
How pleasant to know the air embraces us
whichever way we go.

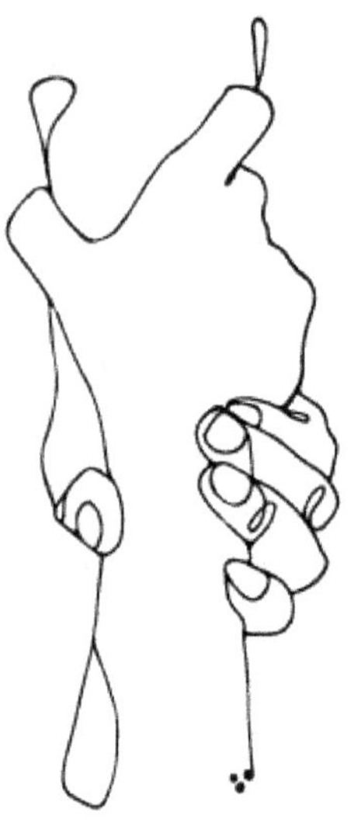

comparison

They constantly orbited each other,
were present in every season.
It seemed they rose and fell in accordance with
each other
whether or not they were on opposite ends of the
universe.
How were they to help the creeping of
comparison?
   "What are you doing?"
"I'm looking at you"
   "What do you see?"
"A reflection."
Their truth.

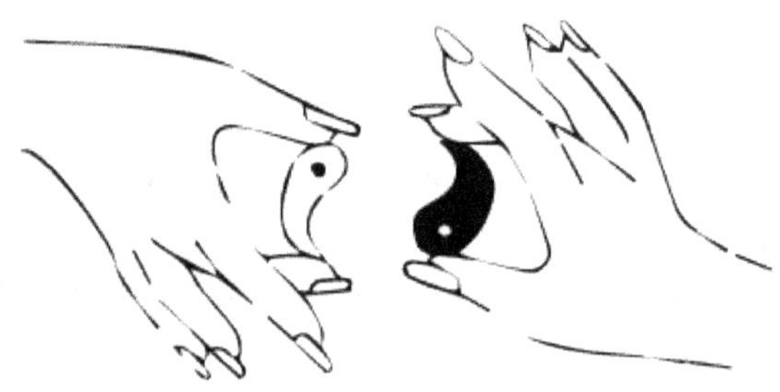

beauty

Narcissus examines his reflection in the lake
until he passes.
The lake weeps not for the loss of his beauty,
but for the loss of seeing its own beauty
reflected in his eyes.
The lake is a teacher.
It does not understand comparison in
competition.
And I have learned beauty is reflected in the
good,
whether or not I am witness to it myself.

love

I love, love.
Romanticizing even the way a plant's vines wrap
around our fences,
claiming our creations as part of their earth,
agreeing to live life together.
What is life,
If not an exchange, a culmination of love against
the forces of the world.
And as I look back at the fading remnants of our
love,
a love that will no longer continue the way it
was,
I can't help but smile.
What a privilege to have brushed past you at that
eminent moment in time
during our grand walk of life.
May we carry our love for others as we part,
everlasting and ever fleeting.

opposition

She both feared and craved opposition, for it had been her one steady
        companion and she didn't seem to know how to live without it.

"I'll pass"

                                        "Why?"

"In this world there are always those who will oppose you. If you're weak, you naturally have opposers of those with more strength, opposing you either as balanced opposites or as a means of trying to prove something. When you're strong, opposers naturally gravitate toward you to challenge that strength. Both instances I've explained are the exact same."

                        "It's because of opposers that I
                                chose to seek you out."

"..."

"Opposers are not something
I'm short on. Does that make me
weak or strong?"

"I suppose that depends on your reaction."

"...."
"And what does your
reaction mean?"

"It means I'll pass."

The road not taken

horror

More, more, more.
I believe I read somewhere once that, in the
horror genre, monsters created for or by men
were more penetrative but those for or by
women were consumptive.

To make your way in or to make it a part of you.
Two sides of the same token, that of which goes
by the name absence. Absence of agency.
Absence of power. Absence of presence.
Absence of "more".

Unapologetic consumption. How subversive
T A K I N G U P S P A C E, auditory wise,
spatially, more than what is told is "for" one as if
it is something to be given.
When you feel everything must be given or
everything is being taken.
Drain, drain, drain.

When air is out of reach, you gasp for more.
Grasping at all to avoid emptiness.
Take and take so you can breathe again.

Why is the air out of reach in the first place?
You shouldn't have to fight for air.
You cry, you shout, but that is tears and voice
drained from you as well.
There is no end. You need more. That is Horror.
The hourglass sand is constantly moving. One
side, always emptier than the other. This you
understand.
More.

In this way is horror simply the bare revelations
of desire? The ugly, raw extremes of existence.
That which invokes fear and releases
characterized monstrous versions of unserving
truths.
What a scary thought indeed.
More.

Dare I say the true absence is love?
How poetic the horror stemming from lack is to
consume into oneself.
For love in a way is integration; unity.
Unsurprising then is the collective lean toward
consumption as a base for more.
More, more, more.

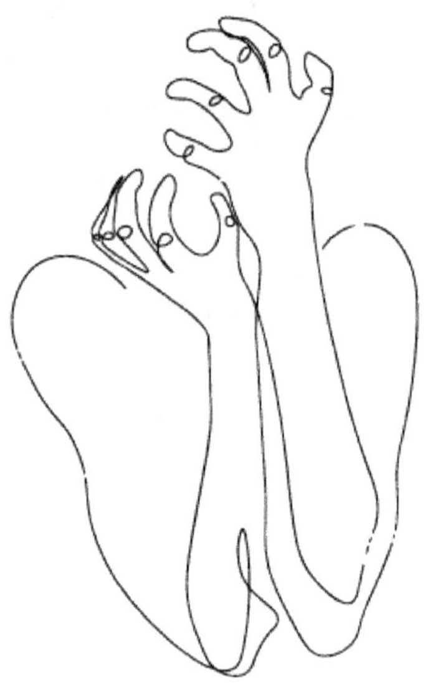

inner child

There's always a little girl outside.
I think she controls the weather.
And every time I'm outside, with no cover, she
makes it rain.
Cold drops pound on my skin with no pause.
I pretend I don't notice and she makes it louder.
My socks are drenched and I walk ever so
carefully along so she cannot hear
the water pressed in my boots.
There's a tension rising, building, banging,
begging to escape.

There's something about being the observer and
observed.
To cause the rain while simultaneously trying to
escape it.
I am the child experiencing and doing, yet I
helplessly watch as she embraces all she feels
and does not yet understand what it means.

She's asking, NO demanding, to be heard
and I don't know why it's so hard for me to listen
to her.
Feel your feelings they say.

Why can't I do it, figure it out?
Never have I ever wished more to know the
seemingly dead language of my soul.

self love

How many times do I need to rearrange all the
words in the world?
How many times can I,
before you realize the desperation I contend with
just to tell you that you are enough for this
world.
And it has never regretted your existence.
For without you,
the snowflakes would have rearranged their
designs
and fell on empty grounds in mourning,
and the cold would've engulfed me in the
loneliness that comes without self love.
How fortunate
we have the power to turn the cold barren winter
into an enchanting land of our dreams.
And I'll rearrange all the words in the world
a thousand times over
so the snowflakes can glisten.

wasted potential

Potential and the infinity that lies between one
second and the next.
Wasted potential and the suffocating feeling that
exists between a breath in and a rest.

A standard unwritten,
a destination untold.
Paths unlimited
and what actually unfolds.

What is wasted potential?
Does it all depend on us?
When there's wasted potential, does it
necessarily mean the potential used isn't
enough?

What makes potential wasted?
Is it the feeling of regret?
The dissatisfaction that lies in our minds,
unkempt.

Can wasted potential mean sadness
for a reality that didn't unfold?

Can it mean success?
Lessons for the current road.

Potential actualized and unactualized.
What a peculiar concept.
A part of our becoming
but why is it we try and measure it?

Mourning who we could've been,
celebrating who we currently are,
looking for what we could be.
A motivation or deterrent?
Potential wasted and what it means.

Alas, wasted potential is something we never
may escape.
But why do we run?
Why do we not take it in an embrace?
For while there's always wasted potential, one
thing never leaves.
That is, in the end, potential's possibilities.

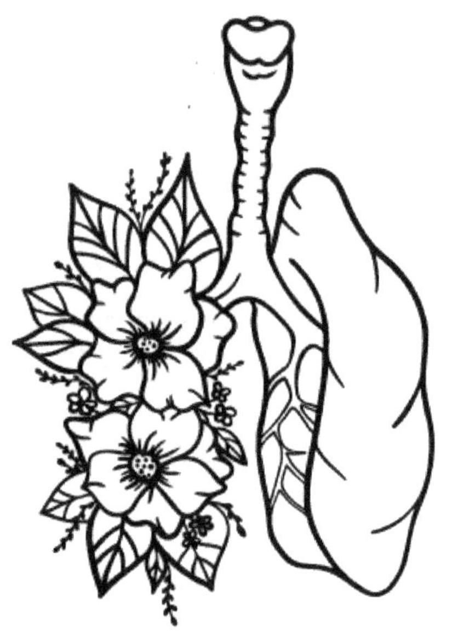

forgiveness

How do you approach forgiveness?
Gentle, blunt, understanding, as a force to be
reckoned with?
How do you approach forgiveness,
for an open wound?
Pain, but the one holding it never intended to
inflict it upon you.
How do you approach forgiveness then?
Knowing its mention will share the hurt you
feel,
not wanting to touch a wound among others
but needing to heal.
Not erasing the reality.
Love strong and hurt fragile; forgiveness an
alloy of both.

existential crisis

Crisis means to sift,
so I pretend my troubles are grains of sand up
against the water,
stars among the vast space of the universe.
And as i sift, I find shells and life and shards and
light and dark and different colors
that transcend beyond my existence yet make up
my essence.
I graze the sharp edges and bask in the warmth
And I find myself amongst it all
and remember to live my life in love.

jaimais vu

I wished with you
that I felt deja vu.
Even this feeling
is welcoming to me.
I wish the world sent a sign to tell me I was
right.
As our lips met,
I did not feel the familiarity of multiple lives,
a home I was coming back to.
I tasted the sweetness of the unknown
and thought maybe this may work out after all.
Jaimais vu.

choose

Flip a coin,
so you don't have to make the decision,
so it's left up to the fates,
so at the end of the day there's no one to blame
but the coin.
Flip a coin,
that only has two sides
embossed with the answer you try to touch with
the tips of your fingers.
Heads or tails?
Tossed and turned
the same as you feel.
Caught.
When you look at the coin
Does it reflect what you want?
Flip a coin, you say
Is that what you deserve?

What is the E word?

What is the word that begins with E?

My essence was summoned to the world tree, this metaphorical organism with endless roots and branches that seep into and reach everything one can imagine and more.

What is the word that begins with E? Is it essence?

I followed the path in the tree; one carved out for me. I did this until I reached my space and my metaphorical alter that had no shape until I gave it one and no significance until I experienced it.
My alter wasn't an item I held dear to me nor did it resemble any emotional ties. Instead, before me lie a sort of seat made of white marble. Hard and cold to the touch at first, until I sat in it and it became a place of peace and comfort. Plush to the touch. It seemed to be a way of transportation as it changed my scenery as my thoughts progressed.

Was the E word escape?

Eventually, I found myself laying in the water, waves soothing me and letting my energy flow as it was meant to. Understanding the need to release what I wasn't aware I was holding. The silence to merely ponder with no expectations. No longer was my mind flitting through different spaces, transporting to try and find something to appease my thoughts. There I think, "I am a part of the tree which is part of everything and therefore with everything I am one". A simple truth it seems.

Is the E word escape? Is it the word everything?

How can it be escape when the reality that appeared was that there's nothing to escape *because* of the word everything. If it's all connected, there's no escaping. It's not escaping when one wants to leave, but merely evolving to include another part. To make another part more prominent, more supported. To notice and nourish something new. The stem stands strong because of the roots. The branches can reach out across infinities because the stem and endless roots support it. The leaves grow and change with the support and changes internally and externally.

I suppose the E word is evolve.

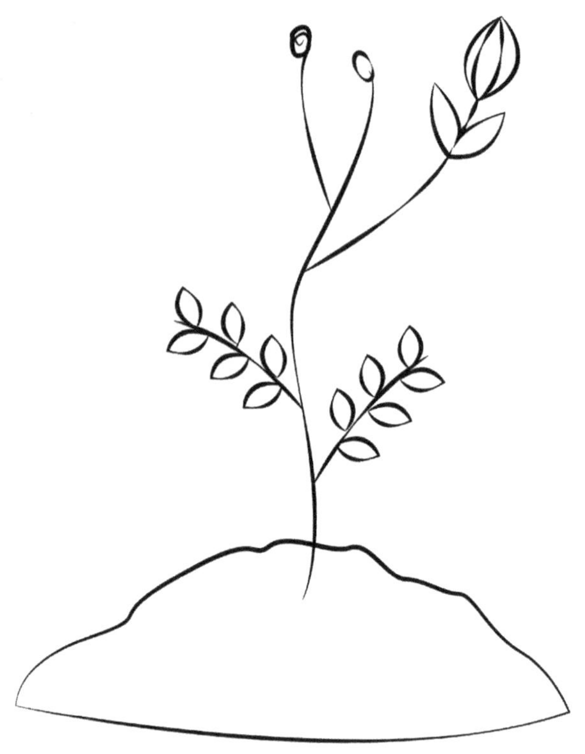

restraint

Sometimes I want to be? or is it to go?
absolutely feral.
To exist in the abyss unrestrained, unconfined.
Even as I pour my thoughts out I remain unsure
and hesitant in wording,
wondering if this is how I want to explain
myself as if I need explaining in the first place.
But make no mistake,
I'm in the ocean and it is me causing the waves.

wishes

I wish to mimic the butterfly.
To become weightless and take flight.
For people to see me as a sign sent for them,
a harbinger of transformation.
But alas, I find i cannot be as simple as the
butterfly
as it goes through its stages,
as it interacts with the people that see it.
To be human is to fail at building the cocoon
a hundred times
until you realize the cocoon was not meant for
you.
And I cannot fly away,
I must walk the path.
But I still wish to mimic the butterfly.

remembrance

A deep red is what I see when I think of
remembrance now.
The bond of the rivers we all hold,
passed from my ancestors to me,
flowing unrelentlessly.
It is here I remember my strength,
my life force.
How dare I forget it in the first place,
the significance that does not diminish though
we all possess it.
This is where I find my memory
and find I can keep going,
even when the world wants me to forget.

A story's end concludes in the middle.

It's late afternoon now
and I've been here for a while,
unable to decipher what you meant.
I've learned the shape of the hills
and memorized the cracks in the concrete
and yet I still don't understand.
I've met the people and know their names,
I know their stories,
I'm part of them now.
But even they could not help.
They told me simply you're different the next day
because of what happened last.

We're due to meet in the evening,
that much I understood.
Except you never told me exactly where

I was supposed to find you.
So I guess I'll climb the mountains next
Or the highest skyscraper I can find,
and yell to the stars I can almost reach
and ask them if I'm blind.
They'll twinkle down to me as best they can
in the midst of all the smoke,
and then it will be morning again.
And I will learn something new
in search of you.

www.ingramcontent.com/pod-product-compliance
Lightning Source LLC
Chambersburg PA
CBHW070606160726
48003CB00005B/2139